The truth is beyond time and space,

The truth is the law of the Cosmos, the law of the Creator, the law of God!

The labyrinth is the pathway that teaches us truth. If we follow it, we will find our way home.

Dr. Beatrice Bartnett

Disclaimer

This booklet does not make any recommendation about medical care, and no statement should be taken as medical advice. We recommend you see your doctor for advice and care of medical problems.

Publisher:

Lifestyle Institute
P.O. Box 4735
Ruidoso, NM 88345

First Edition - December 1995

© **Copyright 1995 by Dr. Beatrice Bartnett**
(Text and Graphics)

All rights reserved.
No part of this publication may be reproduced or transmitted, in any form or by any means, without permission.

ISBN 0-9622182-7-8

Library of Congress Catalog Card Number: 95-82084

Books by the same author:

Auricular Therapy - Theory and Practice

Auricular Therapy for the Therapist

The Key to the Ear

Urine-Therapy - It May Save Your Life

The Miracles of Urine-Therapy (co-author)

Table of Content

What are Labyrinths?	1
The Peace Labyrinth	4
The Path	4
The Peace Labyrinth's Seven Circles	5
The Four Outer Circles	5
The Three Inner Circles	5
The Thirteen 180^0 Turns	7
The Goal	8
A Cross in the Center	8
The Peace Labyrinth's Exit Path	9
Peace Labyrinth Ceremony	14
Purification	14
Blessing of the Ceremonial Site	15
Entering the Path	15
The Journey on the Path	15
The Center	16
The Exit Path	17
The Simple Exit Path	17
The Exit Path of Universal Laws	18
1st Circle - The Law of Cause and Effect	18
2nd Circle - The Law of Correspondence	18
3rd Circle - The Law of Belief	18
4th Circle - The Law of Attraction	18
5th Circle - The Law of Choice	18
6th Circle - The Law of Compensation	19
7th Circle - The Law of Service	19

The Exit Path of Healing	19
The Chakra Exit Path	21
1st Circle - The Crown Chakra	21
2nd Circle - The Brow Chakra	24
3rd Circle - The Throat Chakra	28
4th Circle - The Heart Chakra	31
5th Circle - The Solar Plexus	34
6th Circle - The Sacral Chakra	37
7th Circle - The Root Chakra	40
Closing	42
Other Peace Labyrinth Uses	42
Eye Chart	42
Concentration Exercise	43
Energy Balancing	43
Energy Balancing Exercise	45
Labyrinth's Exit Path Chart	47

What are Labyrinths?

Labyrinths are sacred spaces. They are one of the great mysteries. Labyrinths are tools that have been used for thousands of years. The energy field of these sacred spaces increase the intuition and the connection with the sacred energy often called Creator or God. Labyrinths are windows to the paranormal world.

It is no surprise that in this special time, the time of transition into a new era, labyrinths are surfacing again. Soon we will see how the *Peace Labyrinth* may help us on our journey.

Labyrinths have been used in many cultures and religions. They can be traced back over 3500 years. Some of the places we find them are Peru, Arizona, Iceland, Europe, Crete, Egypt, India and Sumatra. Because of all the changes and transitions we are experiencing right now, there is a new found popularity; an innate guidance toward old tools.

The form and shape of labyrinths may vary considerably from the Classical Seven Circuit Labyrinth to the labyrinth of the Hopi Nation, and from the labyrinth in the Chatres Cathedral in France to the *Peace Labyrinth*. Some labyrinths are round, others are oval or square. Some of them are in the shapes of animals. They are made from stones, hedges and cords. Labyrinths have been painted on paper and cloth, woven into baskets and knotted into carpets. Some are layed stone by stone into a beautiful mosaic. The labyrinth in the Chatres Cathedral in France took twenty-nine years to be build.

The use of labyrinths is as diverse as their shapes. Most often they have been used for personal rituals such as weddings, baptisms and funerals. Celebrations of the seasons, the harvest, and the full moon were a community affair.

A labyrinth is also a metaphor for life. There is only one entrance, one path and one goal. Although most labyrinths use the same path to exit, the *Peace Labyrinth* has a different exit path.

People who walk the path of the labyrinth may experience rejuvenation and often physical, emotional and spiritual healing. Inner peace and contentment are emotions most often related to the walk.

Christians have been using the labyrinth in memory of Jesus' last journey; the stations of the cross leading toward the center. Also the Rosary, a special prayer to the Blessed Mother, may be used during meditation on the path. The *Peace Labyrinth* can be divided so that the full rosary will be placed unto the path.

The Labyrinth's energy is similar to the energy in domes and pyramids. Experiences such as vivid dreams with deeper colors, increased intuition and a feeling of a deeper connectedness are not uncommon. Physical and emotional healing can take place. It is a very personal experience. Some people feel more somber, while others feel rejuvenated and joyful.

Small labyrinths, either on paper or carved into wood, are used for retracing. This exercise can balance and harmonize our energy. If used simultaneously, one on the right side and one on the left side, it will help to balance the brain energy.

The possibilities of the *Peace Labyrinth's* use are many. Additions such as colors, sounds, prayerflags, candles, incense, and chanting may be added to deepen the mystical experience. These additions are not new to celebrations. The elements, the four directions and the beauty of nature have been used for centuries to celebrate life and to give thanks to the Creator. This is one of the common threads in all religions.

Labyrinths are very unique. They help us to connect with the Creator. They help us to focus on our path by harmonizing and balancing our body, mind and spirit.

In this booklet we introduce you to the *Peace Labyrinth*. The form and design were given to us through dreams. Although it differs somewhat from the past designs, its importance and mystical information are extremely valuable for our time and space.

The design, as you will see, tells the truth. It is totally balanced for the new era, as it was for the past and is for the present. Universal Truth never changes. Meditating on the symbols, as explained on the following pages, will open doors to new knowledge and will increase recognition of the truth. Much of that truth cannot be verbalized, it can only be felt deep within.

The *Peace Labyrinth* can be a tool to increase the Universal Consciousness. It increases the peace vibration within and around us. There are many changes coming our way, on a personal level as well as in our surroundings. The labyrinth can help us through this great catharsis. Growth always requires change, expansion, and motion. The more we are connected with the Creator, with God, the easier it will be to go through all the necessary transitions. This connection is the only reliable and stable asset in our life. However difficult a situation we will face, we are never alone unless we choose to cut ourselves off from the love and peace that always prevails in the nearness of the Creator.

We hope this knowledge will help you on your journey and improve your life. May God bless you.

The Peace Labyrinth

The *Peace Labyrinth* is divided into three areas and seven circles. A *path* is leading into the center. This center is often referred to as *the goal*. The *Path* has thirteen (13) 180° turns. Within the center there may be a cross, a Chinese symbol of peace, a candle, or just simply an open space. The *exit path* is leading out through the seven circles.

The Path

There is only one way into the Labyrinth and only one way out; exactly like life. Entering the labyrinth is like a birthing process, a new beginning. As we follow the path of the seven circles, we are reminded of the seven stages in life - newborn, toddler, childhood, adolescence, adulthood, middle age and old age. It also reminds us of the seven chakras.

This path toward the center is filled with meditation and prayer. It takes concentration to stay on the path. In real life it is so easy to get sidetracked, to go off the path. How often do we like to take shortcuts? If we do so, feelings of confusion and abandonment may overcome us. We may feel lost. Yet if we trust the path and follow it, we will always find the center - regardless how difficult the path - regardless how difficult life.

The Peace Labyrinth's Seven Circles

The seven circles represent many different aspects. One of them is the seven stages of our life; newborn, toddler, childhood, adolescence, adulthood, middle age and old age. Although we are a specific physical age, within us we contain all the stages of life. Our spirit, our real existence, is not connected to time nor space.

The seven circles also represent the seven colors of the rainbow, the seven days of the week, and the seven chakras. Our life is always pulsating within this rhythm of seven.

The Four Outer Circles

The seven circles are divided into four outer circles and three inner circles.

The four outer circles represent the outside world. Examples are the four directions; north, east, south and west, and the four elements; air, earth, water, and fire. They represent our material world (what we have, our home and our work), and our surroundings (mountains, lakes, woods, fields and deserts). They also represent Mother Earth.

The Three Inner Circles

The three inner circles represent our inner world; our body, mind, and spirit. As we are moving through the path, we will come closer to the center, to our core, closer

to the true meaning of life, where we finally connect with the Christ within us, with our Creator.

They also represent the family unit; father, mother and child. We are all moving through this family unit; first as children and then as mothers or fathers. All three energies are important to complete this unit. Too often today, one parent is missing. As we start to realize the importance of this family concept, we may start to play a part in another family unit, to complete someone elses trinity, as well as our own. Adopting a family unit will give us a chance to nourish this important human need to be part of a whole.

Within us, we have the energy of a child, of a female (mother, sister) and of a male (father, brother). The concept of being androgynous means being in perfect balance with all three energies. Each one of us is intrinsically unique. Although many of us do not conform to societal standards, if we accept who we are, with all our energies and feelings, we start to become whole. The word holy comes from the word whole, meaning being one with who we are, totally balanced.

The more we live this concept of accepting ourselves, the more we can be a valuable part of our family, our community, the country and humanity.

Another concept of the trinity is time; the past, the present and the future. We do not have a present without a past, and the future is built on the present. They are very closely connected with each other.

Time can only exist within space. Time and space together give us an experience. Without time or space, we would not have an experience. We would just BE. Jesus once said I AM. (Unrelated to space and time, but infinite.)

The labyrinth may help us to reach that I AM experience. Because we are embodied in space and time, we are able only to glimpse that I AM state.

The *Peace Labyrinth* is divided into three equal parts because our life is deeply connected and guided by the concept of three.

The Thirteen 180° Turns

The number thirteen often receives a negative rap. In life nothing is really negative or positive. It just is. Our reaction to something or somebody will make it negative or positive.

The number thirteen occurs naturally around us.

There are thirteen moon cycles each year. The moon relates to the female energy. As we are moving from the male dominated era of the last several thousand years into the aquarian age, we will find that the female energies will become stronger in their expressions. Therefore we will find more balance between the male and the female energies within us and around us.

The number thirteen also appears to be closely related to the Blessed Mother, the Universal Mother, who also is the patron of our Church the *Sanctuary of the Blessed Mother*. She appears around the world from Fatima to Canada and Medjugorjie in the former Yugoslavia, to Christians and non-Christians alike.

Often she appeared on the 13th of the month. Incidentally, without any planing, all our important dates relating to our work occurred on the 13th of the month .

The Goal

In the center we are becoming united with our goal. The circle is representing the Universal Love or Consciousness. Terminology is not important as long as there is a connection with God. Reaching the center is like reaching our goal. It is a place for rebirth. It is a transition into another realm.

A Cross in the Center (optional)

The cross may be placed into the middle of the center. The cross represents the four elements; fire, air, earth and water as well as the four directions; north, east, south and west.

Many Native Americans celebrate Mother Earth and give thanks to the Creator for giving them such a great Mother. She nourishes them, warms them, and provides them with a home for their life's journey.

Many Christians relate their path to a pilgrimage. The station of the cross may be placed on the path. Those who follow the path will meet Christ.

The Peace Labyrinth Exit Path

This exit path is a source of recognition of who we really are. It will give us a chance to fully accept ourselves, to balance our energies, and to become whole again.

In most of the near death experiences, one passes through a tunnel toward a light. Many survivors are talking about the reviewing of one's life. This review is extremely detailed and multidimensional. It deals with the effect of our actions. As an example, Tom has a bad day and is extremely short with Ruth, a co-worker. Ruth feels hurt and past experiences trigger the emotion of anger. A customer calls with a problem and Ruth takes it out on her. I believe you get the picture.

It is like throwing a pebble into a pond. The many circles created have an effect on the whole pond. Each of us is a drop of water within that pond and therefore each of us feels the effects. Together we are the pond. Disturbing the pond with the pebble is like disturbing the quietness, the peace.

Every action and every thought has an effect. Each is like a pebble. By thinking positive, praying and performing good deeds, we create positive motion. That kind of motion creates a positive effect toward a person or community. Remember, it is said that we will receive hundred fold of what we give out.

Unfortunately the same holds true for negative thoughts and angry emotions. It will have an effect on everyone including ourselves.

Passing through the exit path compares to a quick review of life.

As we exit this life we will retrace through the **seven stages of life**; from old age, to middle age, adulthood, adolescence, childhood, toddler, and newborn. As we review our life stages - our good deeds and our mistakes - we will receive understanding of the **truth** without judgement. We will learn to let go and to **forgive** others as well as yourselves, to **love** unconditionally, to have **compassion**, to have **courage**, to have **patience**, and to finally be at total **peace**. Seven attributes, one for each of the circles.

As we exit the labyrinth we have an opportunity to balance our energies. Each of the seven major chakras are connected with a circle. Each chakra supplies energy to specific bodily functions and emotions.

Let me explain briefly for those of you who are not familiar with the chakra system.

Chakras are energy centers. We have seven major chakras and many minor chakras. Every chakra is vibrating on a specific frequency. If a person is out of balance, the frequency is changed. That change will affect the body physically, emotionally and spiritually.

Everything we see has a vibration or a frequency. Color, sound, people, animals, flowers, and all inanimate objects. Our bodies have a general vibration. It is made up of the specific vibrations of each tissue and organ, of each thought, emotion and chakra. Because these vibrations can be measured, some medical tests are founded on this principle.

Many spiritual healers are working with these vibrations as well. They may add an object, sound, color or prayers to the person's energy to balance the vibration.

As an example, if somebody is very nervous and anxious their frequency is much stronger, much more dense. By introducing something like sound, thoughts or color with a specific frequency, the vibrations will unite and the result will be a frequency somewhere in between the two. It is like mixing up two colors. Doing so, we will receive a third color. When we mix blue and yellow together, we will receive green. Why? Because we change the vibration of the colors by combining the frequencies.

Our bodies are surrounded by luminous bodies also called auras. Most diseases have their origin in the aura. Even accidents and surgeries may extend into the auric field. This is the reason why scars may still be painful after 20 years. Phantom pain is another example of this phenomena. Although a limb is lost on a physical level, it still exists on the auric level. Cancer and chronic conditions are interconnected with our energy bodies; therefore healing must occur on all levels. Healing circles, hands-on spiritual healing and art therapy, to mention just a few, are great tools used to reach the auric level.

The aura is divided into seven different bodies. Each of these layers is connected with one chakra and with one of the *Peace Labyrinth's* circles on the exit path.

The auric bodies are as follows (starting from the

denser, inner bodies to the lighter, outer bodies); etheric body, emotional body, mental body, astral body, etheric template body, celestial body and ketheric template or causal body.

The Etheric Body

The first auric body, the etheric body, is related to the 7th *Peace Labyrinth* circle and the base chakra. It is the connection between the physical body and the light body. It contains the same structure and organs as the physical body.

The Emotional Body

The second auric body is the emotional body. It is related to the 6th *Peace Labyrinth* circle and to the sacral chakra. This body is associated with feelings.

The Mental Body

The third auric body is the mental body. It is related to the 5th *Peace Labyrinth* circle and to the solar plexus. This body is associated with thoughts and mental processes.

The Astral Body

The fourth auric body is the astral body. It is related to the 4th *Peace Labyrinth* circle and to the heart chakra. This body is associated with love. It is the doorway to the other realms, to other states of reality. It is the connection between the three lower (physical) auric bodies and the three higher (spiritual) auric bodies.

The Etheric Template Body

The fifth auric body is the etheric template body. It is related to the 3rd *Peace Labyrinth* circle and to the throat chakra. This body is associated with knowledge. It is also a blueprint of our expression in matter and ether. The etheric template body represents the physical level of the spiritual plane.

The Celestial Body

The sixth auric body is the celestial body. It is related to the 2nd *Peace Labyrinth* circle and to the brow chakra. This body is associated with universal connectedness. The celestial body represents the emotional level of the spiritual plane.

The Ketheric Template Body or Causal Body

The seventh auric body is the ketheric template body. It is related to the 1st *Peace Labyrinth* circle or the center. It belongs to the crown chakra. This body contains the lightest vibration and is the closest connection to God in this incarnation. The celestial body represents the mental level of the spiritual plane.

The more we are connected with the Creator, the more we are in tune with the Universal Energy, the more God can work through us. Opening up ourselves to this wonderful healing, loving energy and sharing it with others, is a true blessing.

And always remember, healing is coming from the Creator. We may be the tool, but not the healer.

Walking the exit path one can meditate and pray within each circle. Color, sound, prayerwheels, candles and incense may be added to intensify the experience.

Labyrinth Ceremony

Labyrinths are used in many different ways. The more important the ceremony the longer the preparation takes. If there is not a permanent labyrinth available, part of the preparation is to build one. Often a group of people share in this task as part of the ceremony.

Purification

The beginning of any ceremony is purification. It is a physical, emotional and spiritual cleansing of the participants and the ceremonial site. This may take anywhere from a few hours to days.

Physical Body

We recommend light food the night or the day before. If the ceremony is very important, fasting may be indicated. Please note that not everyone is able to fast. We recommend you consult your physician beforehand. Breathing exercises, t'ai-chi, yoga and meditation will help in this aspect of preparation.

Emotional Body

Take some time and collect your feelings and emotions. Is there happiness, sadness, joy, excitement. Is there confusion, anger, loneliness. Make yourself aware of where you are emotionally.

Spiritual Body

Spend some quiet time of prayer, meditation and relaxation to connect with the Creator. The labyrinth will help to fine-tune this connection. Concentrate on what is really important. This will help you to receive guidance on your journey.

Blessing of the Ceremonial Site

If there is no permanent labyrinth available, the participants are usually building one as a team. After choosing the site, blessings are given in the form of prayers, incense and chanting. The four directions are used as a guide.

Entering the Path

Just before entering the path, incense is used (usually *White Sage*) to purify body, mind and spirit.

The Journey on the Path

The reasons one may journey through the path are infinite. There are walks for blessings, thanksgivings, and forgiveness. Some are walking the path to seek help and healing for themselves, their families and friends. Others are seeking answers to their difficulties and pain.

Some people pass through the path on their knees praying as they go, while others dance through it, celebrating life.

One of the favorite methods is using the prayer walk. It is a slow, meditative walk. Make a fist with your right hand, keep the thumb outside. Place your left hand over your right fist. Place both hands over the solar plexus, (located between the bottom of the chest bone and the umbilicus or belly button). As you take a slow deep breath through your nose, take one step forward, and as you breathe out slowly through your mouth, take another step forward. Do this walk in a very rhythmical, slow and meditative mode.

As you breathe out, release all the tension, all the pain,

sorrow, and sadness that is stored within your body. Release all these emotions with every breath that leaves your body. As these painful emotions disappear, you will have space for other new, positive emotions which are very healing and loving.

As you breathe in, you breathe in this wonderful healing, loving, caring energy, that will permeate every cell in your body. This wonderful energy is the Universal Energy, the God energy. This energy is always available to anyone accepting it.

As you walk slowly, you start to notice that every part of your body feels better, healthier and rejuvenated. After concentrating on your walk for a while put this exercise on *automatic pilot*. You are now ready to connect fully with the God energy and to enter into communion with the spirit until you reach the center.

The Center

The center is the core of the labyrinth. Special ceremonies such as weddings and baptisms are held in the center. It is the place where one can reach the strongest connections and the deepest meditations.

Here are some ideas on how to use this sacred space.

- Use the four directions for prayers.
- Light a candle.
- Light incense and cleanse your body, mind and spirit. Offer it to the four directions with thanks and friendship.
- Have a basket for wishes and messages.
- The content of the basket may be burned during the ceremony or later. Please be aware of any fire danger in your area.

The Exit Path

After walking the path and receiving communion in the center, it is time to leave the labyrinth through the exit path.

This process can be done in a very simple way, or more elaborately with chimes, prayerwheels and meditations.

The Simple Exit Path

As you exit the labyrinth through this specific path you will cross all seven circles in a straight line. By doing so you are crossing through the seven stages of life. You are crossing through your meditations and prayers, through your thoughts and emotions that you have experienced on the path going in. As you are passing through all these energies, you may send out this wonderful warm light that you have received in the center.

Your thoughts may be concentrated on being grateful for having had communion with your Creator, for being blessed with this opportunity to find inner peace.

The Exit Path of Universal Laws

This exit path takes a little longer than the simple exit path. A meditation within each circle will open us up to universal laws and truths.

The more we are in harmony with these laws, the more we understand them and make them an integral part in our lives. By understanding and living the universal laws changes can be made to influence life positively.

Here are some examples of laws that can be meditated on:

1st Circle - The Law of Cause and Effect

We live in an orderly universe in which everything happens for a reason. There are no accidents.

2nd Circle - The Law of Correspondence

As within, so without: your outer life will tend to be a mirror-image of your inner life.

3rd Circle - The Law of Belief

Whatever you believe becomes your reality.

4th Circle - The Law of Attraction

You inevitably attract people, events and circumstances into your life that harmonize with your dominant thoughts.

5th Circle - The Law of Choice

You are always free to choose the content of your conscious mind, but in so doing, you are choosing every other part of life.

6th Circle - The Law of Compensation

You are always fully compensated for whatever you do, positive or negative.

7th Circle - The Law of Service

Your rewards in life will always be in direct proportion to the value of your service to others.

The Exit Path for Healing

A special healing meditation within each circle will ready the heart, the soul, the spirit and the body to receive healing. There are two kinds of miracles. The first ones are the results of a change within us. The second ones are a grace from the creator.

Healing does not always mean getting cured. Miracles and healing can occur on all levels.

Meditate on the following thoughts and say the affirmation 3 times aloud.

1st Circle

Healing is a basic human function and is the result of inner harmony, peace and love.

Affirmation: I am a child of God and therefor always loved and cared for. All is well.

2nd Circle

Healing is a process and not an event. It is a daily exercise of balancing body, mind and spirit.

Affirmation: Every part of my body works in perfect harmony. My Body, mind and spirit are perfectly aligned. All is well.

3rd Circle

Healing is rarely convenient. Emotional, physical and spiritual changes will occur which may cause pain and fear on all levels.

Affirmation: Change opens new doors. I am always protected. There is nothing to fear. I am well.

4th Circle

Healing means to make whole; to accept and embrace all parts of yourself; all the parts you love and all the parts you hate.

Affirmation: I accept and love myself right now, exactly the way I am. All is well.

5th Circle

If you cannot be in the stage you love, love the stage you are in. Live in the moment, enjoy and celebrate life.

Affirmation: I love the stage where I am. I feel surrounded by light and love at this moment. All is well.

6th Circle

Healing follows no timetable. It is an expression of inner harmony and peace.

Affirmation: I am surrounded by loving thoughts and beautiful light. All is well.

7th Circle

Every illness is a message, listen and you will hear.

Affirmation: I am loved and guided at this very moment and always. My life is filled with joy and peace. All is well.

The Chakra Exit Path

Those of you who are aware of your body's own energies know how beneficial it is to balance the chakras. Those of you who just started to learn about it are in for an expanding experience. The more you are in tune with yourself and the Creator, the more you will feel your own energies and the energies around you.

The chakra path starts in the center and follows a straight path through the labyrinth. On the path you will pass through a total of seven circles (including the center one). Poles can be erected where the circles meet the path. Paint the poles with the appropriate color (see later), and add the chimes with the specific sounds (see later). Add the attributes for each chakra in the form of a prayerwheel or a flag. A candle may be placed at each position; also a basket for messages and offerings.

The chakra path starts in the center and is walked after the labyrinth ceremony. With both eyes closed, the weight balanced on both legs, both hands on the side and palms out, take a deep breath through the nose. Imagine with every breath that a pure white light is entering your body. After a few breaths, the whole body will be filled with this wonderful, pure light - this warm, loving light energy.

Now you are ready to experience the exit path.

1st Circle - The Center
The Crown Chakra

Slowly move toward the pole that belongs to the crown chakra. Stand in front of it and ring the chime. Let the vibration of the sound, a B-sound, interact with your body.

Place your hands in front of your abdominal area and imagine you are holding a ball of white light. Feel that ball in your hands. Push this ball of white light into your stomach and move it all the way up into your head and out through the top of your head. Stretch out your arms as you are finishing the push and turn your palms outward, giving this wonderful white light back out into the universe. Slowly bring your hands down to where you started. Repeat this process two more times. You may change the color from white to violet if you wish.

Take a look at your prayerflag or prayerwheel. What you see is the Chinese symbol for peace. Meditate on that symbol for a while. What does peace mean to you? How do you manifest peace in your life?

Peace

Peace is related to the crown chakra because, within the essence of God, within the center, there is pure peace.

Peace begins deep within yourself. It requires total trust and faith in God. It requires a connection with the Creator. If you let yourself be guided by God there will not be space for fear, or anger, or the need to fight. You learn to let go and trust. Out of that trust, peace is born. If you are peaceful within yourself everything around you will become peaceful.

Peace can be a reality if you make it a part of your life experience. Everyday anew you must connect to God in order to learn trust.

Light a candle or put a message or an offering into the basket for peace.

Special prayers or chants may be offered at this time.

How does the 1st circle influence you?

Spiritual Effect

The crown chakra is the connection between the Universal Consciousness and your own spiritual being. It is the bridge to the paranormal. Alignment of the crown chakra is the catalyst to recognizing the past, the present and the future as it pertains to your life. This includes past life experiences. Being in the 1st circle will help you to accept who you really are, so you can fulfill your spiritual purpose in life.

Emotional Effect

You have finally come home. You have a deep feeling of connectedness, of love, and of peace. Nothing really matters except being a part of this circle, being a part of the Creator. That is why the center is often called *the goal*. Missing the connection with this circle will give you a feeling of homelessness, a feeling of being lost and unloved. The emotional pain will be tremendous and will definitely have a negative physical effect.

Much of this pain can be seen within society. Addictions of any kind are signs that people long for such a state of peace and well-being. Yet it can only be found deep within - through meditation, prayers and the grace of the Creator.

Physical Effect

The crown chakra balances brain functions (especially left and right brain synchronicity) and the central and peripheral nervous systems. Conditions such as addictions, nervousness, and hyperactivity may be seen as a sign of imbalance. Also all skeletal problems, including subluxations of the spine, are related to the crown chakra. The major gland controlled by the crown chakra is the pineal gland.

Remedy

Concentrate on peace. Balance the crown chakra through deep meditations, prayers, and chanting. Use white and violet light. Use the B-chime, and carry stones with you such as Amethyst, Flourite and clear Quartz. Walk the labyrinth as often as you can.

First thing in the morning and last thing at night connect to your Creator. Ask for guidance and protection. The more you connect, the stronger the relationship between you and the Creator becomes.

The strength and peace you receive through this relationship will carry you through life, through good times and difficult times. You will never be alone.

2nd Circle
The Brow Chakra

Slowly move to the 2nd circle and stand in front of the pole. This circle is related to the brow chakra. The brow chakra is located just above the middle of the eyebrows. It is also the location of the third eye. Ring the chime and let the vibration of the sound, an A-sound, interact with your body.

Place your hands in front of your abdominal area and imagine you are holding a beautiful ball of indigo light. Feel that ball in your hands. Push this ball of indigo light into your stomach and move it all the way up into your head and out through the top of your head. Stretch out your arms as you are finishing the push and turn your palms outward, giving this wonderful indigo light back out into the universe. Slowly bring your hands down to where you started. Repeat this process two more times.

Take a look at your prayerflag or prayerwheel. What you see is the Chinese symbol for patience. Meditate on that symbol for a while. What does patience mean to you? How do you manifest patience in your life?

 Patience

Patience is one of the hardest attributes to learn.

It means giving up your own agenda and timetable and accepting whatever comes at whatever time.

It takes a lot of trust to let go and let things happen. Sure, sometimes actions are necessary. But too often you just do not have the patience to wait until all the pieces are coming together, so to speak.

Fate has an interesting way of teaching you patience. It may present you with a long term disease or other difficult situations over which you have no control. You can fight it or you can flow with it. Often the worst disasters bring out the best in people such as compassion, caring, and patience. It is your decision alone how you will look and react to a situation.

If your own agenda is the only important aspect in life, you will miss out on what really counts.

It requires patience to meditate and to pray, to be quiet, to feel and to listen. Yet in this quietness, you will find the connection to the Creator, and through that connection will come answers and guidance.

The Creator is guiding you daily on your path. It is up to you to accept this help by being patient and waiting for the proper timing. When you put away your agenda and follow the more important higher agenda you will receive peace.

Animals are a wonderful example. They are so patient when waiting for their masters and their love is unconditional. They are wonderful teachers.

Light a candle or put a message or an offering into the basket for patience.

Special prayers or chants may be offered at this time.

How does the 2nd circle influence you?

Spiritual Effect

The brow chakra is connected with the third eye. Opening this chakra will increase your creative visualization and your spiritual visions. It will connect you with the realm of clairvoyance. Dreams may become more intense and colorful. Also they may be filled with guidance and information.

Emotional Effect

Patience is an attribute that stimulates self-esteem and security. Truth and understanding will be shown to you when you are patient enough to wait. Sometimes it takes years to finally understand the good that may have come out of tragedy. As you experience patience in your life you learn to just go with the flow and to accept hardship, disease, and pain as something temporary. Everything is always changing. You cannot hold on to anything, nothing is static. The connection with your Creator will carry you. It is the life-line that carries you through the river of life.

Physical Effect

The brow chakra is in charge of the autonomic nervous system. The ears, eyes, and nose as well as the endocrine system (especially the pituitary gland) are all connected to this energy center. Some parts of the immune system are strengthened by a balanced brow chakra.

Remedy

Balance the brow chakra through meditations, prayers, and chanting. Concentrate on patience. Use an indigo light, use the A-chime, and carry stones with you such as Lapus Lazuli, Sodalite, and Flourite. Walk the labyrinth as frequently as possible.

Try every day to have more patience with family members, friends and co-workers. If you see the good in every person and realize that every person is an expression of the Creator, it will be easier to show acceptance, love and patience.

3rd Circle
The Throat Chakra

Slowly move to the 3rd circle and stand in front of the pole. This circle is related to the throat chakra. The throat chakra is located just below the Adam's apple. Ring the chime and let the vibration of the sound, a G-sound, interact with your body.

Place your hands in front of your abdominal area and imagine you are holding a ball of blue light, a wonderful, brilliant blue light. Feel that ball in your hands. Push this ball of beautiful blue light into your stomach and move it all the way up into your head and out through the top of your head. Stretch out your arms as you are finishing the push and turn your palms outward, giving this wonderful blue light back out into the universe. Slowly bring your hands down to where you started. Repeat this process two more times.

Take a look at your prayerflag or prayerwheel. What you see is the Chinese symbol for truth. Meditate on that symbol for a while. What does truth mean to you? How do you manifest truth in your life?

Truth

Truth is a big word in society. Everybody likes to know the truth about what is going on. Yet truth does not have anything to do with rules and regulations, with the laws of the land, or with who is right and who is wrong.

Or the opposite may be true; all those rules and regulations may have little to do with the truth.

Truth is an expression of the Cosmic Laws, of the Universal Laws. The laws of cause and effect.

What are some of those truths?

- Love is the connecting energy between all creation.
- Death does not exist, it is merely a change in form.
- All people are created from spirit and are equal regardless of color, creed, nationalities or religious beliefs.
- Just because something cannot be seen or is not known, does not mean it does not exist. Two hundred years ago it was only a dream to fly and travel throughout the world. Two hundred years from now, the same may hold true for intergalactic travel or time travel.

The truth you have to follow is the Universal Truth. The more you are connected, the more you will receive guidance and will know what is right and wrong.

You will be judged not by the standards of people or nations, but by the Universal Laws.

Any action can effect hundreds of people. If the action is a positive one, you will receive a positive reaction. The same is true of a negative or painful action. It will effect hundreds of people and eventually it will return to you hundredfold.

Living in accordance with the Universal Truth will make you righteous. It will give you inner peace and strength.

Try to learn more about truth and how you can express it in your life.

Light a candle or put a message or an offering into the basket for truth.

Special prayers or chants may be offered at this time.

How does the 3rd circle influence you?

Spiritual Effect

The balanced throat chakra can give you insight into the Universal Truth. It will increase your understanding of spiritual laws. By understanding and following these laws you may manifest abundance in your life. Telepathy is also strongly related to the throat chakra. It is the understanding and knowing of mind and thoughts of people, animals and plants.

Emotional Effect

Realizing Universal Truth may cause conflict with old values and learned knowledge. Standing up for truth may alienate you from the world you have been living in, from friends and family. You may even become a social outcast. There were many great spirits who spent their lifetime in prison because they stood up for the truth. Every sacrifice for truth, regardless of size, has a direct effect for bringing about change.

Conflict may cause pain and separation. Many of you are living with this separation every day. Balancing the throat chakra will help you to follow your inner guidance. By connecting to the Creator you will receive the strength and the know-how to live within the truth.

Physical Effect

The throat chakra balances the mouth, teeth, gums, the esophagus and the vocal cords. It is also tied to the respiratory system and part of the alimentary canal. The major gland effected is the thyroid.

Remedy

Balance the throat chakra through deep meditations, prayers, and chanting. Use blue light, use the G-chime. Use stones such as Turquoise, Tourmaline and any stone that contain light blue color. Walk the labyrinth as often as possible. All these exercises will help to balance the throat chakra and to find the truth.

4th Circle
The Heart Chakra

Slowly move toward the pole that belongs to the heart chakra. Stand in front of it and ring the chime. Let the vibration of the sound, an F-sound, interact with your body.

Place your hands in front of your abdominal area and imagine you are holding a ball of green light. Feel that ball in your hands. Push this ball of green light into your stomach and move it all the way up into your head and out through the top of your head. Stretch out your arms as you are finishing the push and turn your palms outward, giving this wonderful green light back out into the universe. Slowly bring your hands down to where you started. Repeat this process two more times.

Take a look at your prayerflag or prayerwheel. What

you see is the Chinese symbol for love. Meditate on that symbol for a while. What does love mean to you? How do you manifest love in your life?

愛 Love

The love consciousness is directly related to the opening of the brow chakra. The more you increase your love capacity, the more your third eye will develop.

There are many forms of love. The love of a child for a parent. The love of a parent for a child. The love of a child for another child. The love between a man and a woman or between a woman and a man. And the love of a person for God. Yet the most important of all is the love of the Creator to his creation.

This love that you receive from the Creator is always around you and within you, regardless of the fact that you may loose sight of it for a while or that you may feel unworthy of being loved. The Universal Love is always with you.

The more you realize that you are a child of God, and you are loved, cared for, and provided for, the more loving you become in your own relationships. Love can move mountains. Anything is possible because of love. Every life expression you see is a creation of God. God is Love, therefore love is expressed through all living things; every person, every animal and all plants. Are you treating all living things with the same love and respect?

Love can be expressed in many different ways. A couple of hours spent with somebody who is lonely, a smile, or a tap on the shoulder may be all that is needed to let them know that they are not alone.

Every minute of your life you make the decision to be positive or negative, to be loving and caring or indifferent. You make the choice and you live and feel the effects personally, as well as within your family and community.

Every day is a new day to exercise this awareness, to be loving and caring in the image of the Creator. The more you exercise it, the better you get at it.

Light a candle or put a message or an offering into the basket for love.

Special prayers or chants may be offered at this time.

How does the 4th circle influence you?

Spiritual Effect

The heart chakra is connected to love. Opening this chakra will increase the caring for your brothers and sisters, and caring for yourself. With love comes compassion and healing. The more balanced and in-tune the heart chakra is, the stronger the Universal Energy can work through you. Spiritual healing and hands-on healing are flowing strongly through this chakra. It takes love to develop and strengthen your relationship with the Higher Power.

Emotional Effect

Everyone is in need of love. Love is a flow of energy from one creation to another. Opening yourself to receive and to give love will connect you with the circle of love. Love is to humans what sunshine is to a flower. It is needed for growth and to become your best. Not receiving love will create feelings of loneliness and low self-esteem.

Physical Effect

The heart chakra is closely related to the heart and circulatory system. It helps in the rejuvenation of tissues, the thymus gland and the immune system.

Remedy

Balance the heart chakra through deep meditations, prayers, and chanting. Use a green light and the F-chime. Use stones such as Rose Quartz, Amethyst, Tourmaline and any stone that is green in color. Walk the labyrinth frequently.

Every day try to give love to somebody special; a smile, a helping hand, or whatever your inner guidance is telling you to do. All these exercises will help you to increase your capacity for love and will balance your heart chakra.

5th Circle
The Solar Plexus

Slowly move toward the pole that belongs to the solar plexus. Stand in front of it and ring the chime. Let the vibration of the sound, an E-sound, interact with your body.

Place your hands in front of your abdominal area and imagine you are holding a ball of yellow light. Feel that ball in your hands. Push this ball of yellow light into your stomach and move it all the way up into your head and out through the top of your head. Stretch out your arms as you are finishing the push and turn your palms outward, giving this wonderful yellow light back out into the universe. Slowly bring your hands down to where you started. Repeat this process two more times.

Take a look at your prayerflag or prayerwheel. What you see is the Chinese symbol for forgiveness. Meditate on that symbol for a while. What does forgiveness mean to you? How do you manifest forgiveness in your life?

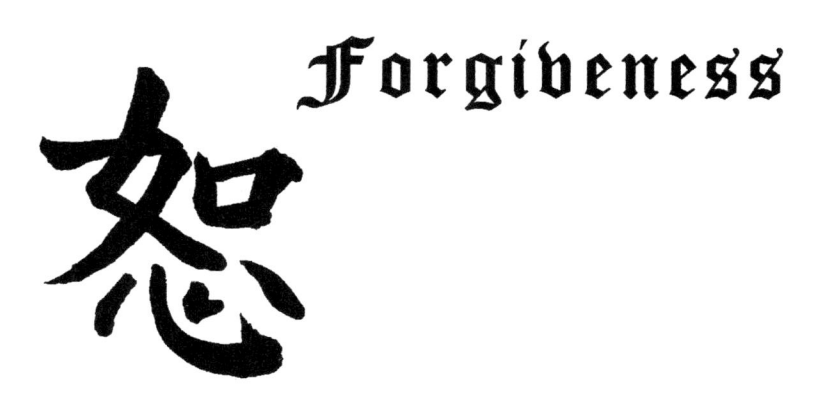

𝔉orgiveness

恕

Forgive and let go. This is one of the basic principles for growth and happiness. Every emotion and every thought takes up space within your body. This space is limited. If you choose to fill it with anger and emotional pain, there may not be any space left for positive and loving emotions. What you have to learn is to forgive any pain and hurt you have received. To forgive does not mean to forget. It means letting go of the pain and anger that is attached to the memory.

Forgiving yourself is probably one of the most difficult tasks. Often you feel you do not live up to the expectations of other people such as parents and friends. Therefore you feel you are not worthy to be loved and will deny yourself that privilege.

Accept yourself right now, the way you are, and not the way you believe you need to be.

The Creator does not make junk. You are a wonderful creation, and have a wonderful spirit. You have so much to give and to teach, and so much to learn and to experience.

Every day is a new day for a new beginning. Remember all humans make mistakes. This is alright, as long you try your best.

Light a candle or put a message or an offering into the basket for forgiveness.

Special prayers or chants may be offered at this time.

How does the 5th circle influence you?

Spiritual Effect

The solar plexus is the chakra for happiness and spiritual joy. It strengthens the intellect. By letting go and forgiving, the spirit is becoming very light. The solar plexus is also the attachment of the silver cord that connects you with the outer realms. This cord is used for astral travel and is always connected to the body.

Emotional Effect

Having a balanced solar plexus will give the emotion of joy and happiness. A feeling of freedom is also very closely connected. An imbalance of this chakra causes feelings of limitation and depression.

Physical Effect

The stomach, the digestive tract, the liver and the gallbladder are all tied to the solar plexus. The absorption of nutrients plays an important role in today's health and is also tied into the solar plexus. The major glands connected with this chakra are the adrenals.

Remedy

Balance the solar plexus through deep meditations, prayers and chanting. Use yellow light. Use the E-chime. Use stones such as Citrine, Topaz, and stones which contain yellow color. Walk the labyrinth frequently.

Forgive yourself right now and let go. Accept yourself they way you are today, this minute. Be always grateful for the gift of forgiveness and enjoy every minute of your life.

6th Circle
The Sacral Chakra

Slowly move toward the pole that belongs to the sacral chakra. Stand in front of it and ring the chime. Let the vibration of the sound, a D-sound, interact with your body.

Place your hands in front of your abdominal area and imagine you are holding a ball filled with orange light. Feel that ball in your hands. Push this ball of orange light into your stomach and move it all the way up into your head and out through the top of your head. Stretch out your arms as you are finishing the push and turn your palms outward, giving this wonderful orange light back out into the universe. Slowly bring your hands down to where you started. Repeat this process two more times.

Take a look at your prayerflag or prayerwheel. What you see is the Chinese symbol for compassion. Meditate on that symbol for a while. What does compassion mean to you? How do you manifest compassion in your life?

慈心 Compassion

Compassion is love and patience in action; feeling the pain and suffering of another person and sympathizing with him or her.

This requires sensitivity. It requires one to become still and just feel. The more you are aware of your own feelings, the more you can feel the emotion of other people. The sacral chakra allows you to connect on the emotional level to people, animals and plants. Being able to feel compassion will increase the feeling of togetherness, brotherhood and sisterhood. Unity is the result of action built on compassion.

Light a candle or put a message or an offering into the basket for compassion.

Special prayers or chants may be offered at this time.

How does the 6th circle influence you?

Spiritual Effect

The sacral chakra is connected with sensation and feelings. It controls personality traits and offers optimism, self-confidence and enthusiasm.

Emotional Effect

This chakra deals with personality emotions. An imbalance in this chakra may create an over-importance of the physical and sexual energies. The person will exhibit a self centered lifestyle. Detoxification on an emotional level will help to balance the sacral chakra. Nervousness is common. Balancing this chakra calms and relaxes a person. This will help the healing process.

Physical Effect

The sacral chakra is tied to the muscular system as well as the spleen, bladder, and the kidneys. Elimination through the urinary system, the colon, as well as the skin is the big key here. It helps to detoxify the body. The less toxic you are on a physical level, the more the energy can flow. The major glands related to this chakra are the spleen and the pancreas.

Remedy

Balance the sacral chakra through deep meditations, prayers, and chanting. Use orange light. Use the D-chime. Use stones such as Carnelian, Citrine and all stones containing orange color. Walk the labyrinth frequently.

All these exercises will help to balance the personality and bring about spiritual, emotional and physical growth.

7th Circle
The Root Chakra

Slowly move toward the pole that belongs to the root chakra. Stand in front of it and ring the chime. Let the vibration of the sound, a C- sound, interact with your body.

Place your hands in front of your abdominal area and imagine you are holding a ball of red light. Feel that ball in your hands. Push this ball of red light into your stomach and move it all the way up into your head and out through the top of your head. Stretch out your arms as you are finishing the push and turn your palms outward, giving this wonderful red light back out into the universe. Slowly bring your hands down to where you started. Repeat this process two more times.

Take a look at your prayerflag or prayerwheel. What you see is the Chinese symbol for courage. Meditate on that symbol for a while. What does courage mean to you? How do you manifest courage in your life?

英 **Courage**

Courage is the ability to stand up for the truth, to swim against the flow when necessary, and to take the more difficult road when required.

For some people it takes courage to get up in the morning. Every step may be a very difficult and imposing task. While for others courage may mean to save a child from a dangerous situation.

Some people are scared of one thing and others of something different. Whatever fear you have, you can always overcome it and go beyond. The more you overcome fear, the more you learn to trust in your own abilities and the guidance of the Higher Power. You will learn that the strength will be there in times of need.

Light a candle or put a message or an offering into the basket for courage.

Special prayers or chants may be offered at this time.

How does the 7th circle influence you?

Spiritual Effect

The root chakra is the site of the Life Energy, the force for survival. It can conquer fear and promote courage. If this Life Energy is connected through all seven major chakras it will bring the person to new spiritual heights. It is the site of the kundalini energy.

Emotional Effect

If the root chakra is balanced, there will be a strong feeling of connectedness to the Higher Power, to the infinite Life Force. If this chakra is not balanced, there may be insecurity and jealousy. Basic questions such as *who I am?* may be asked. It also deals with emotional survival.

Physical Effect

The root chakra is tied to the gonads, the fight and

flight response, the pelvic area, and the legs and feet. Reproduction is related to this chakra.

Remedy

Balance the root chakra through deep meditations, prayers, and chanting. Use red light, use the C-chime, and use stones such as Smoky Quartz and all stones containing red color. Walk the labyrinth frequently.

All those exercises will balance the base chakra and will turn this wonderful energy into a tool for courage.

Closing

After you have finished the seven circles and are leaving the labyrinth, turn around and face the center one more time.

Give thanks to the Creator for the experience as you connect your hands, palm to palm, in front of the heart chakra and bow your head in respect.

Other Uses for the Peace Labyrinth

The uses of the *Peace Labyrinth* are limited only by your imagination.

Here are some of the ideas.

Eye Chart

Get a large version of the *Peace Labyrinth* and hang it up on the wall. The chart position should be eye level when in a sitting position. Sit in front of the eye chart, six to ten feet away, and follow the path slowly with your eyes. Do not move your head. Repeat this exercise three times. This will strengthen your eye muscles. Like any form of exercise repetition is the key. Once or twice daily is recommended.

Concentration Exercise

Get a large version of the *Peace Labyrinth* and hang it up on the wall. The chart position should be eye level when in a sitting position. Sit in front of the eye chart six to ten feet away. Take a deep breath and breathe out all the tension in your body, mind and spirit. Repeat the deep breaths a few times. Make sure your spine is straight so the energy within your body can move up the pathways located in your back.

Now concentrate on the peace symbol located in the center of the *Peace Labyrinth*. Focus all your attention on this symbol. If your mind wanders, refocus. Do not fight any thoughts that may enter your mind and distract you. Consciously accept these thoughts and place them into a waiting area in your mind. Try to concentrate for ten minutes every day. The more you do this exercise the better you get at it. It will become easier.

This will help you to focus on whatever you wish to do in your life. The stronger your ability to focus the more you are able to create reality.

Energy Balancing

This exercise will balance the energy between the right and the left side of the brain. Take a look at the drawing on page 45. When you turn the book 90^0 counterclockwise you will find two *Peace Labyrinths* side by side. You will notice the right one is mirrored. Tracing the right and the left paths together will help to balance the energy within your system. Follow the direction below and repeat the process a few times daily.

Make yourself comfortable, sitting or standing at a table. Take some deep breaths. Relieve all your physical, emotional and spiritual tension as you breathe out. Breathe in the wonderful Universal Energy that will heal you, love you and enlighten you. If you feel relaxed you are now ready to trace the *Peace Labyrinths*.

Take your index fingers and follow the paths slowly. Try to move simultaneously. As you move your fingers concentrate on the energy that is created by the movements of your hands. The more often you do these movements, the more you will develop a flow to the point that you move without a guide. Then you are ready to do this exercise anywhere. Move your hands right in front of you and follow the imaginary *Peace Labyrinth*. As you do this you are creating a strong energy field. Healers who do this exercise before an energy cleansing or healing work may be amazed at the results. This exercise balances the energy and lets one be a greater vessel and conductor of the Universal Energy.

After experiencing the Peace Labyrinth first hand, take this knowledge and use it for the benefit of mankind. The more you are using it as an integral part of your life, the more you will enjoy the blessings that come with it.

Write us with your experience and ideas. One day we will meet and celebrate the Labyrinths together. Until then, may God bless you.

Energy Balancing Exercise

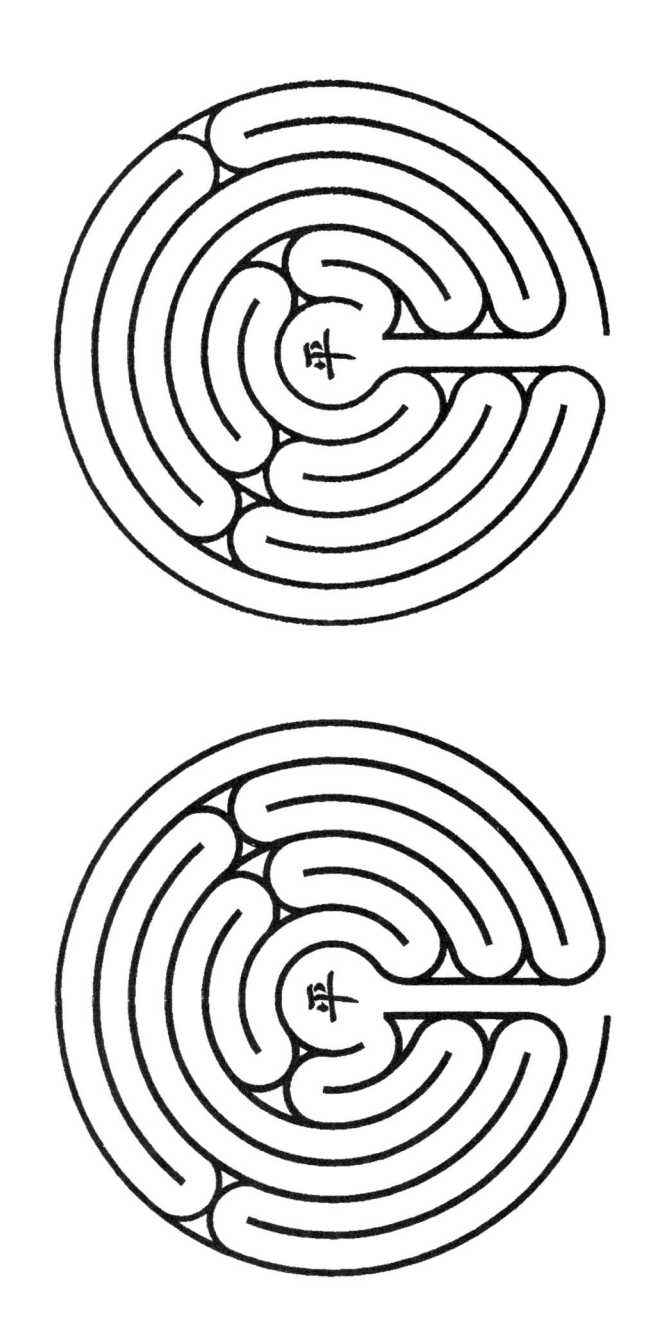

Notes:

Labyrinth's Exit Chart

Position	Chakras	Chakra Location
Center 1st Circle	Crown	Top of head.
2nd Circle	Brow	Just above the middle of the eyebrows.
3rd Circle	Throat	Just below the Adam's apple on the throat.
4th Circle	Heart	In the upper 1/3 of the chest bone.
5th Circle	Solar Plexus	In the middle between the umbilicus and the chest bone.
6th Circle	Sacral	Just below the umbilicus.
7th Circle	Root	Base of the spine.

Labyrinth's Exit Chart

Position	Life Stages	Color	Sound
Center 1st Circle	Old Age	White Violet	B
2nd Circle	Middle Age	Indigo	A
3rd Circle	Adulthood	Blue	G
4th Circle	Adolescence	Green	F
5th Circle	Childhood	Yellow	E
6th Circle	Toddler	Orange	D
7th Circle	Newborn	Red	C

𝕷𝖆𝖇𝖞𝖗𝖎𝖓𝖙𝖍'𝖘 𝕰𝖝𝖎𝖙 𝕮𝖍𝖆𝖗𝖙

Position	Crystal & Stones	Attributes	
Center 1st Circle	Amethyst Flourite Clear Quartz	Peace	平
2nd Circle	Lapus Lazuli Sodalite Flourite	Patience	忍
3rd Circle	Turquoise Tourmaline all blue stones	Truth	孚
4th Circle	Rose Quartz Amethyst Tourmaline all green stones	Love	愛
5th Circle	Citrine Topaz all yellow stones	Forgiveness	恕
6th Circle	Carnelian Citrine all orange stones	Compassion	慈
7th Circle	Smoky Quartz and all red stones	Courage	英

Labyrinth's Exit Chart

Position	Body Systems	Astral Bodies
Center 1st Circle	Brain Synchronization	Ketheric Template or Causal Body
2nd Circle	Autonomic Nervous System	Celestial Body
3rd Circle	Respiratory System	Etheric Template Body
4th Circle	Circulatory System	Astral Body
5th Circle	Digestive System	Mental Body
6th Circle	Elimation Systems	Emotional Body
7th Circle	Reproductive System	Etheric Body

NOTES:

Order Form

Please send me ____ copies of the book

Urine-Therapy - It May Save Your Life!

Enclosed is a check or money order for $ 9.95 per book ($ 9.95 for the book plus $2.50 s/h). NM residents please add 6.8125 % sales tax ($ 0.68 per book).

Name _____

Address _____

City, State _____ ZIP _____

    send to: Lifestyle Institute
                     P.O. Box 4735
                     Ruidoso, NM 88345

Order Form

Please send me ____ copies of the book

The Miracles of Urine-Therapy

Enclosed is a check or money order for $ 13.95 per book ($ 11.95 for the book plus $ 2.50 s/h). NM residents please add 6.8125 % sales tax ($ 0.82 per book).

Name _____

Address _____

City, State _____ ZIP _____

    send to: Lifestyle Institute
                     P.O. Box 4735
                     Ruidoso, NM 88345

Peace Labyrinth Kit

**Build your own *Peace Labyrinth*.
Easy instructions
and tools included.**

Please send me the following kit:

_____ 45' Peace Labyrinth Kit

_____ 27' Peace Labyrinth Kit

Enclosed is a check or money order for $ 99.00 per Kit. Add US $ 7.00 s/h. NM residents please add 6.8125 % sales tax ($ 7.29 per kit). Please ask for international shipping rates.

Name _____

Address _____

City, State _____ ZIP _____

send to: Lifestyle Institute
P.O. Box 4735
Ruidoso, NM 88345

This is the basic Peace Labyrinth without the exit path additions.

Order Form

Please send me
Super Blue Green Algae Information

Enclosed is a check or money order for $ 2.00 per package. NM residents please add 6.8125% sales tax ($ 0.14 per package).

Name _____

Address _____

City, State _____ ZIP_____

    send to: Lifestyle Institute
                    P.O. Box 4735
                    Ruidoso, NM 88345

Stay informed with the
Lifestyle News!

THE LIFESTYLE NEWS is a quarterly publication for people interested in alternative and non-traditional healing methods. It is published by the Lifestyle Institute.

If you are interested write to:

        Lifestyle Institute

        P.O.Box 4735

        Ruidoso, NM 88345

A yearly subscription is $ 12.00, for Canada US $ 14.00, and other countries US $ 16.00 (outside US - only check or money orders drawn from a US bank in US funds). NM residents please add 6.8125% sales tax ($ 0.72 per subscription).

SANCTUARY FOR HEALING AND PEACE

The time has come for the manifestation of our vision. An alternative village containing a Sanctuary for Healing and Peace, including a seminar center and a home for children, pregnant women and battered women.

This village will be on several acres in New Mexico consisting of geodomic houses (round houses).

Our work can be defined as helping people to find inner peace, guidance and strength. We believe that the answers to our problems, physical, emotional and spiritual in nature, are within us. If we reconnect to the higher power, bathe ourselves in that higher energy, then the path for our growth and healing is revealed, problems solved and often diseases disappear.

Our healing center will include alternative therapies, for physical, emotional and spiritual healing. They range from t'ai chi, art, music and counseling to body work, lymphdrainage, detoxification, nutrition, herbs, chiropractic, fasting, steam and water therapies, energy balancing and many more.

Our seminar center will be a special place of learning – a practical experience of healthy, peaceful, and balanced living. Classes and seminars on many different subjects and cultures are planed.

Our home for children, pregnant women and battered women will be a safe heaven and a place of growth, love and caring.

Our Sanctuary will be an oasis of peace, love and healing.

For more information on this project, or any help you may offer, please write to:

Sanctuary of the Blessed Mother
P.O. Box 4735
Ruidoso, NM 88345

About the Author

Dr. Beatrice Bartnett, D.C., N.D. was born and educated in Switzerland. Being exposed to alternative healing at an early age, it was only natural for her to enter the field of Naturopathy. After her studies in Germany, she practiced as a Naturopathic Physician in Switzerland.

In the early 1980's, Dr. Bartnett came to America to study Chiropractic. She holds a degree from Life Chiropractic College in Georgia. In 1987 she earned her Doctorate in Naturopathy.

A pioneer in alternative healing methods, especially Auto Therapies, Dr. Bartnett has done extensive research and has lectured in India, Europe, Central America, the Caribbean Islands, Canada and the USA. She has been on radio and television in several countries.

Dr. Bartnett has authoredsix books and numerous articles and pamphlets. One of the books has been translated into several languages. She is the editor of the quarterly newsletter, the *Lifestyle News*. In 1991, Dr. Bartnett founded the Lifestyle Institute.

Dr. Bartnett practices at the Ruidoso Health Institute in New Mexico. She has developed a new approach to prevention and recovery of today's health conditions. It is a combination of nutrition, naturopathic bodywork, lymphdrainage, auriculotherapy, detoxification, stress control, exercise and body, mind and spirit balancing. Dr. Bartnett sees patients from all continents for intense healing work in Ruidoso. She also offers phone consultations and retreats.

Dr. Bartnett's vision includes a Sanctuary for Healing and Peace, a seminar center and a home for children, pregnant women and battered women.